My Body Belongs to Me was created to help children develop
a healthy self-concept and feel good about their body. Respect
for their body and the understanding that their body belongs to
them can empower children if they are threatened with potential
sexual abuse or exploitation. This book presents the following safety rules:

- Say "No" in a loud voice.

- Move away to a safe place.

- Tell a grown-up who can help.

My Body Belongs to Me may be used by parents or teachers to
discuss with children what they can do if an adult touches parts
of their body in a way which the child doesn't like or feels is
wrong. It should be emphasized that if a child isn't able to say no
or move away, telling a grown-up who can help is still very important.

My Body Belongs to Me is used with *BodyRights—A DUSO Approach
to Preventing Sexual Abuse of Children* (Circle Pines, Minnesota:
American Guidance Service, 1986).

My Body Belongs to Me

by Kristin Baird

Illustrated by Inese Jansons

AGS ®
American Guidance Service
Circle Pines, Minnesota 55014-1796

Design by Steve Henning, Henning & Associates

Illustrations by Inese Jansons

© 1986 AGS® American Guidance Service, Inc.

No part of this publication may be reproduced
or transmitted in any form or by any means
without written permission from the publisher.

Printed in the United States of America

Originally published as part of
the *Parents and Teachers Can Help* (P.A.T.C.H.) program
© 1984 by Kristin Baird.

Library of Congress Catalog Card Number 86-071361

ISBN 0-88671-173-8

To Bridget, Lesley, and Hillary
so that you and children everywhere
can feel safe and strong.

I have a body.

It belongs to me.

I can do many things with my body.
I can run, jump, throw a ball,
hug, and even sleep.

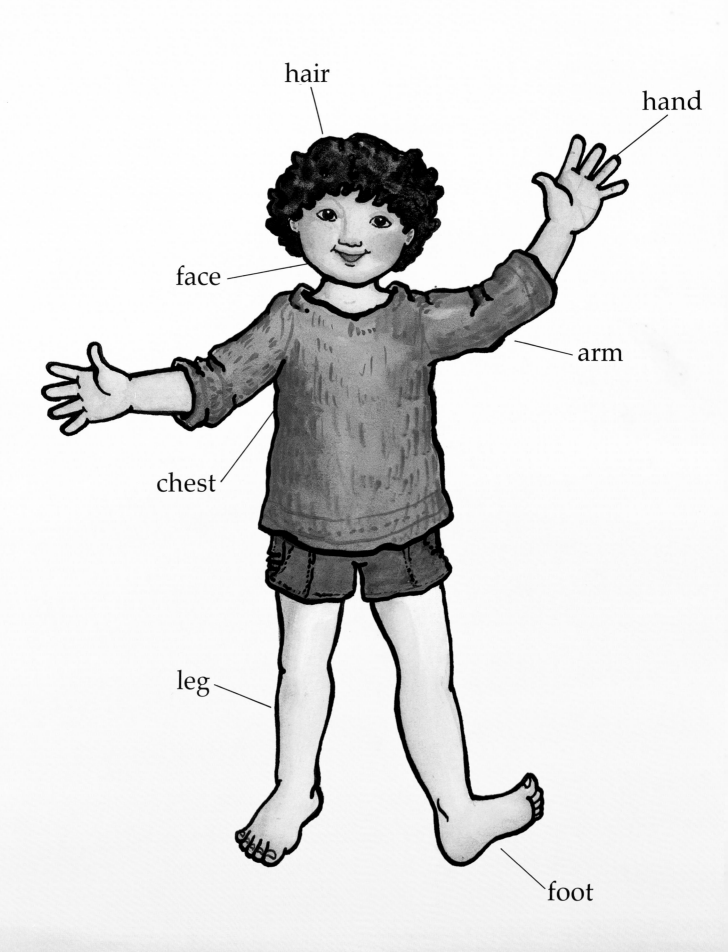

hair

hand

face

arm

chest

leg

foot

My body is made up of many parts.

When I was little,
I learned the names of all my body parts.
I can say all their names.

Do you know the names of your body parts?
Can you say them?

Sometimes, people make up
other names for body parts . . .

. . . like calling fingers "pinkies,"
or toes "tootsies."

These are pretty silly names.

It's important to know the real names
for all your body parts.

Can you say them again?

All of us have the same body parts:
We have eyes and ears,
legs and arms, fingers and toes.

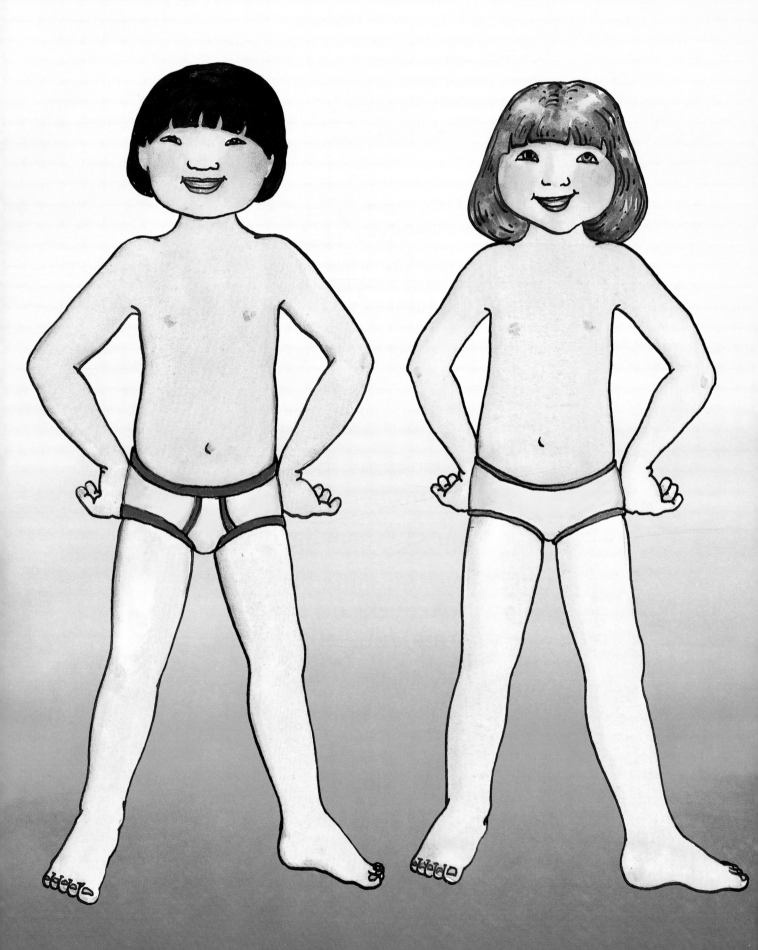

But did you know
that boys are different from girls?
Girls and boys
have different private parts.

Private parts are the parts of your body
covered up by your bathing suit or underwear.
They're called private
because they are usually covered up
and not seen by others.
You don't share your private parts
with other people,
except when you're taking a bath,
or visiting the doctor for a checkup.

Can you think of any other times
when you might share your private parts?

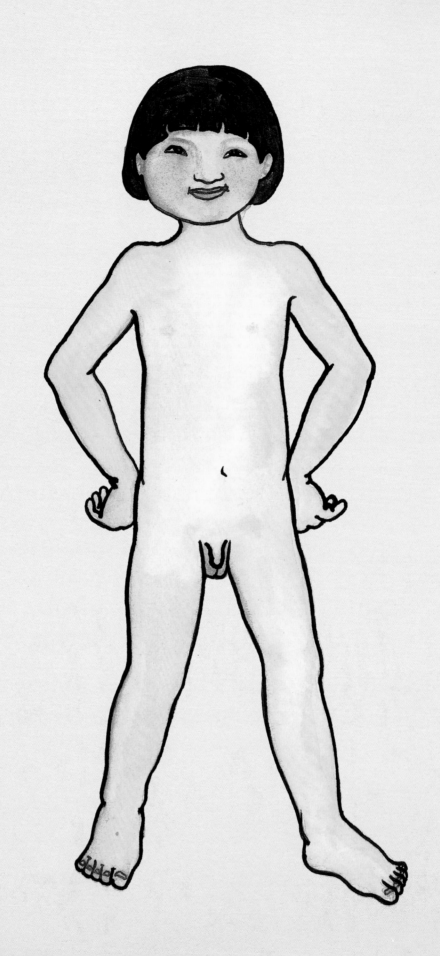

Just like our other body parts,
it's important that we know the names
of our private parts.

Boys have a penis and scrotum.

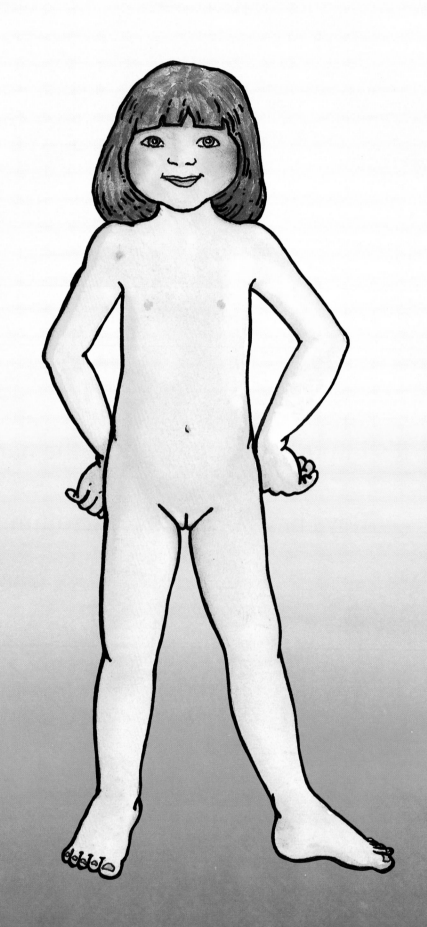

Girls have labia and a vagina.

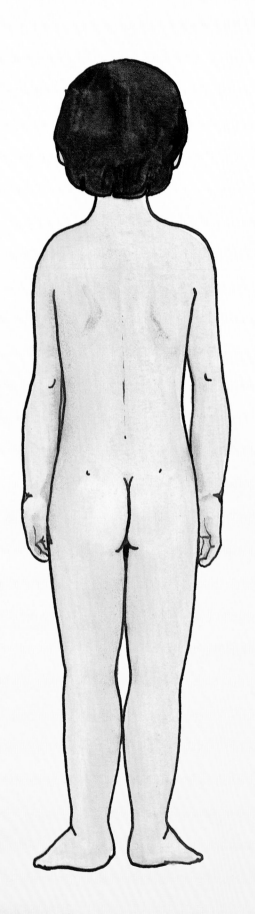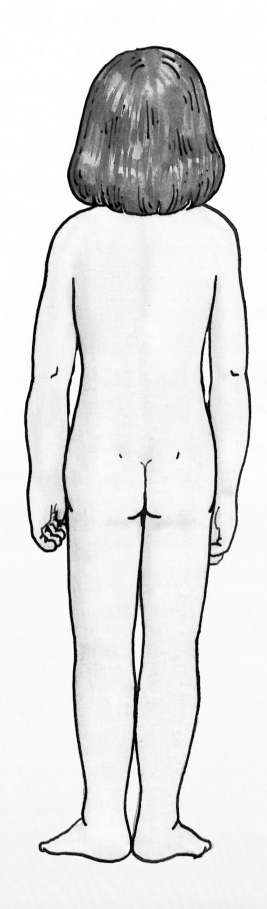

And did you know
that girls and boys have some private parts
that are the same?

Both boys and girls have buttocks
—which we sometimes call a "butt"
—and an anus.

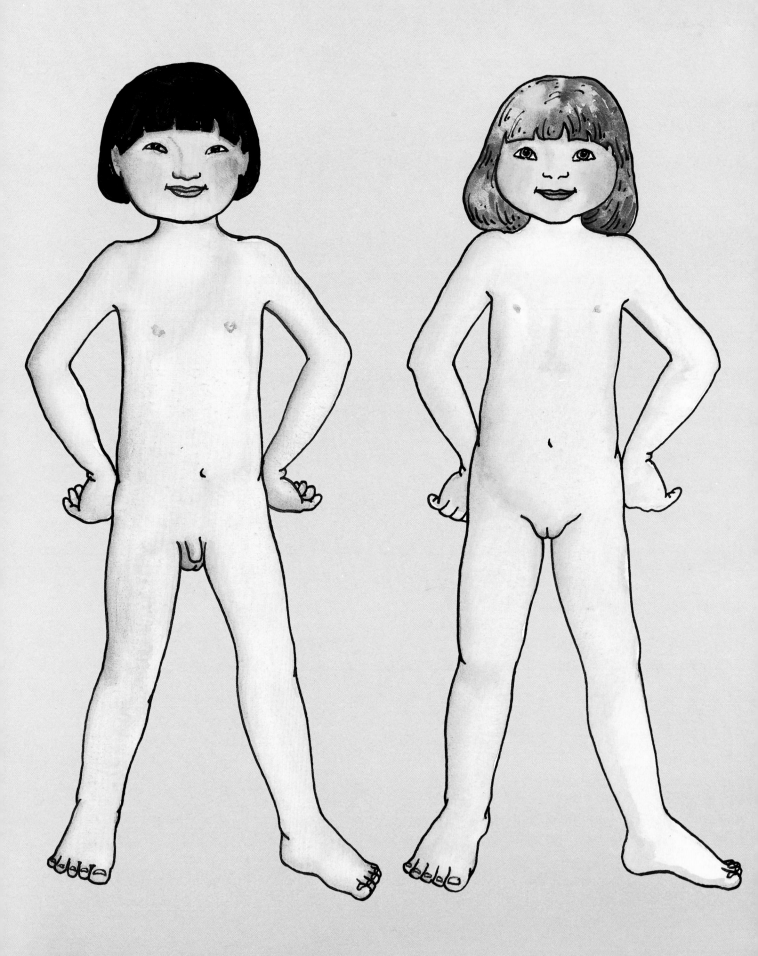

Sometimes people make up
silly names for private parts, too.

But it's important to know
the real names of all our body parts.

I can say the names of all
my body parts.
Can you say the names of yours?

All my parts together
make up my body.

My body belongs to me alone.

I can share my body . . . if I want to.

I can use my arms for hugging
. . . if I want to.

I can use my lips for kissing
. . . if I want to.

But when I don't want to share my body,
I say "No!" in a big voice.

Can you say "No!" in a big voice?

If someone tried to touch my private parts,
I would say "No!"

I would say no and get away to a safe place.

I would say no . . . and get away. . .
and then I would tell someone about it.

I would tell a grown-up who could help.

And do you know what?

I feel safe!

. . . Because I know what to do.

Kristin Baird, R.N., B.S.N., received her bachelor's degree in nursing from the University of Wisconsin and is now a master's candidate in education. For four years she worked as a public health nurse with primary emphasis in maternal/child health. In her professional work, Kristin has been involved with identification and reporting of sexual abuse victims. She has also served as a school health consultant for Head Start, preschool, and K-12 students. Kristin is currently health promotion coordinator for Fort Atkinson Memorial Hospital, and the mother of three children.